THESE TEARS TELL HALF THE STORY

TRE' BROWN

<u>*These Tears Tell half The Story*</u>
Tre` Brown

TEARS

Written By

Psalmist Bara7al

~ MAYBE I WAS NAIVE ~

Maybe i thought you would be different

Maybe i thought i was enough for you

Maybe i trusted you too soon

Maybe i was naive

I mean the way you left me to die while i was bleeding on the floor looking in your eye trying to find the same energy you said you had for me

I mean the way you made me feel so confident in your clouds of falsehood slowly choking me while i enjoyed every last breath

I mean the way i'm here only to wonder how i couldn't convince you to love someone who clearly loved you

I mean the way i'm here crying knowing your eyes are dry

Vulnerability is defined as the quality or state of being exposed to the possibility of being attacked or harmed, either physically or emotionally. These Tears Tell Half the Story contains a series of poetry and stories written as therapeutic mechanisms to heal and to exhale toxicity, pain, trauma, heartbreak, grief, and brokenness. This collection of work has collaborations with poets all over the United States of America who use their gift in order to tell their stories through their creative and innovative lenses.

By the end of the book, you as the reader, will be able to see that it's okay to have feelings and to hurt. This project was designed as a public diary, allowing you as the reader to tap into the minds of not only other poets, but people who have stories to tell and those who have a voice that has been silenced for far too long. You as the

READER WILL ALSO DIVE DEEP INTO MY HEART AND MIND, UNDERSTANDING AND RECOGNIZING THAT EVEN I TOO AM NOT PERFECT BUT A BEAUTIFUL AND AMAZING INDIVIDUAL.

THIS BOOK IS DEDICATED TO THE ONES WHO HAVEN'T HAD THE CHANCE TO SPEAK BUT ARE GIVEN A VOICE THROUGH THE ELEMENT OF STORYTELLING AND SPOKEN WORD. YOU ARE IN FOR AN INCREDIBLE EXPERIENCE. THE SPOKEN WORD AND STORIES ARE WRITTEN IN AUTHENTIC FORM INCLUDING USAGE OF EBONICS (SLANG) AND WILL NOT BE ALTERED IN ANY WAY, SHAPE OR FORM.

THIS BODY OF POETRY ALLOWS YOU AS THE READER TO REMEMBER THAT VULNERABILITY IS STRENGTH AND IT'S OKAY TO BE BOTH MESSY AND ACCEPTED. THESE TEARS TELL HALF THE STORY WILL HAVE YOU CRYING, CLAPPING, SMILING AND ALLOW YOU ACCESS INTO A WORLD WHERE TRANSPARENCY WILL NOT CAUSE ANYONE TO JUDGE OR RIDICULE

YOU FOR YOUR PAST DECISIONS OR CURRENT THOUGHTS.

It's HEALING TIME.

Lee's Prayer

Dear God
I come to you with a heavy heart
I know that you know that
From the very start
You said in your word that I can come
to you anytime
You've given me strength
And shown me why I need you to survive
But it's been hard for me Father
My heart's been broken and shattered
I want you to rise
So that my enemies can be scattered
You helped me to make it through the
night
Now I'm stronger by the day
I put my faith and confidence in You
And trust You always
No matter the situation
Or the trials this world may bring
I'm safe in Your Arms
Where I am able to lean
Everlasting Father
I choose to live for You

To serve You
To live and die for You
And if I be lifted up from the Earth
I'll draw all men unto You
I believe in You
I acknowledge You always
It's in Your Name
That I'll continue to give You the praise
God I'm asking that You hear me and heal me
I hate this brokenness
I hate the depression I'm facing on the inside
But I'm glad You rescued me from wanting to commit suicide
And that's more than enough reason to give You the Glory
I can sing this song of praise because You opened doors for me
I confess
That I'm not perfect
I've sinned
But I need You to save me
I know Your Son died for me

Set me free of my iniquities
Bring me to the Promise that You have
for me
I love you
I honor you
I give you all the honor and praise
In Jesus Name I pray
Amen.

THESE TEARS... TELL HALF THE STORY
The Preface

Sometimes I wonder why I took this long to let these tears out.

I sit

I write

I cry, yell, and scream

Waiting for God to answer me

Man. I forgot to introduce myself, well you know who I am already.

Here we are again. This time, it's personal. This time, I lay my flaws, my pain, my shame, and my hurt at the feet of Jesus through my poetry.

Y'all know how my books go.. Some love, some sad poems, some poetry about God and then some revolutionary things, but this time, this time it's more personal. I'm going to open up and give you vulnerability in human form. I'm taking off the mask and pouring out my heart like a drink

OFFERING. THIS IS GOING TO BE DIFFERENT. NOW, YOU'LL SEE A LOT OF SLANG BUT THAT'S ALRIGHT.

These Tears Tell Half The Story.

WHEN YOU READ THIS BOOK, PLAY IT OVER SOME INSTRUMENTALS. TURN MY POETRY INTO MUSIC. SING OR RAP THE POEMS IN A WAY WHERE YOU CAN CONNECT TO ME. I WILL ALSO ADD THAT THERE ARE NO POEMS THAT SUGGEST DEFAMATION, SLANDERING, INSULTING, OR DISRESPECT. THIS IS MY RELEASE. THIS IS THE WAY I AM ABLE TO HEAL. COME WITH ME ON THIS JOURNEY. THESE TEARS ONLY TELL HALF THE STORY. WAIT, I DIDN'T EVEN TELL YOU WHAT I MEANT BY THAT.

DEPRESSION HAS TAKEN OVER MY LIFE SINCE 2012. I KNOW WHAT YOU'RE THINKING. HOW CAN I BE A MAN OF GOD AND ABLE TO POUR LIFE INTO OTHERS WHEN I'VE BEEN EXPERIENCING DEPRESSION? IT'S TRUE. DEPRESSION IS REAL. IT STARTED WHEN I WAS IN COLLEGE. AFTER BEING TOLD TO KILL MYSELF, I ACTUALLY ATTEMPTED. I HAD 14 SUICIDE ATTEMPTS AND TO BE HONEST, I STOPPED GOING TO THERAPY BECAUSE I COULDNT BEAR TO ALLOW the therapist to give me "tools to heal" when healing is a process.

No one can tell you how to heal. But on this journey, I found myself falling deeper in love with God and certain things had to shift. I lost friends, lovers, jobs, and I even lost myself in the process. However, I've discovered that for healing to take full control, there must be a period of dying. Now, I'm not saying physical death, I'm talking about Dying with the flesh. Your flesh has to die so that you can mature and grow into the person you want to be. You have to give yourself and your plans to God (for those that believe in him) and remember that there's nothing too hard for Him.

My biggest problem was that in those tears I've cried, I should've gone to God instead of social media. I was looking at all these posts on Instagram and Facebook in order to find some comfort, when I should've been in prayer.

These tears tell half the story.

You know, I've discovered that tears are a good thing. Tears help you to see clearly. Tears help you to see clearly. Tears wash out debris from your eyes. Tears help you to release, detoxify, eliminate emotional damage, and destroy significant numbers of stress.

I've cried and made some decisions that were careless, but God reminded me of my purpose and who I am. These tears made me stronger. These tears made me powerful. These tears gave me a new lease on life and now I can stand here confidently knowing that greater is indeed coming.

Okay, enough of my preaching and what not. Are you ready? Are you ready for this experience? Let's go. Let's go to work!

Welcome to my heart.

Welcome to my mind.

Welcome to my world.

Welcome to my life.

This guided and curated experience is brought to you by every emotion that I left on these pages.

I dedicate this book to a muse who no longer wants anything to do with me. Please know that I've never slandered your name or defamed you in any way, shape, or form. I love you and I pray the very best for you. I hope one day we can be friends again.

— Lee "Tre'" Brown, III (Pyro) (Tre'Maine Rashad)

The Prolific Poet © 2022

THE ALTAR I PRAY TO

WHEN I PRAY

I LAY PROSTRATE BEFORE GOD

LOOKING FOR AN ANSWER

GIVING OVER MY BURDENS AND TRANSGRESSIONS

I GO TO THE SOURCE

KNOWING HE'S THE SOURCE OF MY STRENGTH

AND HE SEES ME FOR WHO I AM

ALLOWING HIM TO MOLD ME

FORM ME

AND SHAPE ME INTO WHAT HE WANTS ME TO BE

HE DOESN'T JUDGE ME

HE ACCEPTS ME

WHEN I GO TO THE ALTAR

I GIVE HIM EVERYTHING

THIS ALTAR I PRAY TO

I COME TO HIM BROKEN

KNOWING WHERE MY HELP COMES FROM

READY FOR HIM TO FIX AND RESTORE ME

I go to the altar a hot mess

Lips moving but not allowing anyone to hear me speak

It's me and Abba

Having a conversation

Expressing my frustration

Holy Spirit moving

Satan trembling under my feet

I discovered a renewed joy

Standing in victory

Walked into freedom

Received clarity and my release

Reminded that no one can separate me

From His Promise and His Glory

This altar I pray to

Became the poem

That gave birth to my breakthrough

Because God made a way

He keeps on blessing me

And he's not through with me yet.

Delayed Not Denied
(A Conversation With Simba)

Sometimes

The best inspiration

Comes from the deepest parts of us

Because in doing so

While you write

God could be using you

To bless someone

To help someone who may be going through the same thing

That you're going through

Sometimes

I believe that God gives hard battles

To his toughest soldiers

Cause the devil can't do nothing to you

Unless God allows it

He would only allow it

Cause he knows you can handle it

Unfortunately

We don't know what that something is

But God does

It's to prepare you for what's best

And never to fail you

I know from experience

Depression can sometimes feel inescapable

You'll become content with the lies

Adhere to the dark thoughts in your mind

You wonder if living is worth it

Knowing the hurt you've endured

Is making you second guess yourself

That was me for the past five months

Yes, I confess

Because of heartbreak I've endured

I questioned if I should still be alive

I was losing my mind

Felt like I was running out of time

Wanting to overdose because I overdosed on not letting go

Avoided all the red flags and signs

Made excuses to keep the sparks alive

Looked foolish and disgusting

Appalling and hideous to a major degree

I had to look in the mirror

And ask if this was truly me

Man

I looked a hot mess

It hit me

You gotta know that there's a God in heaven

Who is capable

What appears impossible to the world

God reminds you that He's able

You may feel like you're being delayed

But you're never being denied

You may feel like you're struggling

But God is by your side

The struggle doesn't last forever

You may want to give up

Have gave up

But you're not down for the count

You're not a failure

You're worthy and deserving

Of having your place at the table

Keep going and keep the faith

Even when dark roads lie ahead

God is near to the broken hearted

He's your Father and your Friend

God will bring you through the toughest storms

While you're freezing

He's there to keep you warm

Feel what you're feeling now

You're human

If you're asking God for a way out

He's going to do it

On His Time

In due season

Don't stop believing

Don't belittle your worth or existence

You've been put on this earth with purpose

And to live with purpose

Listen

I know the pain gets tougher

You want to feel appreciated and accepted

By everyone

Truth is

Everyone is not for you

Everyone doesn't have your best interest

However god has a bigger plan

That will give you a brighter future

And a promising tomorrow

I'm never going to tell you to not feel what you're feeling

Never going to tell you to suck it up

I'm telling you to feel every last feeling

That you're feeling

Pain isn't there to hurt you

Pain is there to mold you

And bring something out of you

What you feel now

When God blesses you

You'll be able to look back

Thank and Praise Him

For bringing you out of that dark place

And smiling knowing that you don't look like

What you've been through

A delay never means that your breakthrough isn't coming

A delay is preparing you for what's next

A delay means help is on the way

A delay means get in position for your miracle

Hold that head up

Keep going

You're more than a conqueror

You're royalty

You belong here

Tears don't make you weak

They make you strong

Blessings cannot be denied

To the ones who continue to try

Say I "shall live and not die"

So I wrote this poem

Because I had to speak this over me

The best inspiration came from the deepest parts of me

Now that this poem is complete

And I've gotten my release

Now I can declare

That I am free.

A Letter To My Former Self

Featuring: Acacia M. Taylor

Typically you'd tell your former self
"Slow down"
"It's okay"
"Things will make sense"

That's cute.
But my former self walked through hell
Feet burning from the pain of brokenness
Friendships.
Family.
Love.
My feet have trekked
Across betrayal, malice, lies
My back has carried the weight off my world
Her world.
His world.
The world of those who swore they loved me
Swore that unconditionally they'd walk through the hurricanes with me
I'm walking through the hurricanes on my own
Their words were my levees
And just like Katrina
They lied
Swore i'd be okay
Swore they'd be there
But carefully.
Crack!
Strategically
Crack!
Quietly.
Crack!
The betrayal built
Until my levees could be broken by a simple touch.
A touch that let the floods in
Left me to walk this very hurricane I'm still in
The hurricane they swore to protect me from

From the hurricane
To the fire I was raised in
See, my former self?
We've been through it all
We made it through
Babies i watched slip from me
A heart that's been obliterated
Scars that only my eyes can see
Only my soul knows
My former self, I love you
For the space you hold for those you loved,
Holding space for those who threw you aside.
Just to turn around.
Wait
I need you.
Holding space for the man who left you at 3
Never being able to understand how you love a man
Who was the first to hurt you.
Holding space for the man you bore your soul to.
My former self
You're a force to be reckoned with
For nobody knows pain
Sorrow
Anguish
As you
From the fire you grew.
You've walked in hurricanes
Embraced your own storms
Slept
Found peace
Made a home
In the very storms others gave to you
You made it.
For that,
I bless you
I'll forever adore you
I'll hold space in my soul for you.
For you helped me to grow.
Allowed me to bloom

Gave me these vines
Blessed me with the lushest leaves
Here I am
Having blossomed through the fire
Born again in my own hurricanes
To you
Unconditionally
A letter to you. © Acacia M. Taylor 2022 (5/31/22)

Dear former self
Take the losses
But remember you didn't lose
You're learning
Progressing
Acknowledging that it's okay to make mistakes
You don't have to live up to your parents expectations
They'll support you no matter what
You must keep going.

Dear former self
Not everyone is deserving of you
There will be people who show love
People who initiate hate
Men that will betray you
And women who'll reject a date
But that's a part of life
Be focused on the bigger prize
Don't get distracted
Remember you're a king
No one can take away your crown.

Dear former self
You've had worse days
Give yourself credit and grace
You're stronger than before
Let them think you're weak
Stop putting yourself down
No need to be a people pleaser
Let God be your healer

Let Holy Spirit be your teacher
You don't need to end your life
Because of one setback
What will that do?
Don't you know you belong here
Yes,
The cantankerous sins of not having a mentor hurts
Friends will become your enemies
And will delight to see you hurt
But that's the gift of life
Because you'll see who's for you
And who's not
Former self,
There's royalty in your veins.

If you're going to make a change
Change for you
Kick people pleasing out the window
You belong here
Suicide ain't the answer
Love will heal all wounds
Believe in yourself
And others will believe in you too
When you look in the mirror
What do you see?
Rich melanin and divine energy permeating your body
No shades of ugliness
Only natural light
You're wonderfully made
Self.
You're a gift to humanity
 Self.
No more toxic energy is allowed to consume you
Self.
Only positive vibes from here on out
Self.

Dear former self
Wake up
Put a smile on
You made it
I praise God for you
Hold space in my heart for you.
Praying for you
So as you get older
You'll look back
See what was
Then celebrate that these tears were only half the story.
Dear former self
It's a new day
Seize it
Do what you love to do
This is your world
Don't drop it.

Unconditionally signed
A letter to me. © Tre Brown (5/30/2022)

The Devil Said I'm Reckless

September 14. 2001

Breaking news!

I was selected to be Student of the Week

After waiting weeks and weeks

Watching everybody having a spotlight on them

It's finally my time to shine!

Me

One of 7 Black boys in Ms. Joseloff's class

Getting his due respect

Me

Someone who still needed to figure out

What I wanted to be when I grow up

Eager to tell my classmates my story

Me

The "Pastor" in the class

Before I even decided

That would be my career path

Remembering how much I loved Jesus

Thankful that my parents instilled in me

A relationship with God

Me. Yes, me!

Excited and filled with joy

I sat at my kitchen table

Filled out my "about me" poster

Wanted to stay up on a weeknight

So that i can watch BET Uncut

Me.

I had to go to bed soon

I'm terrified of nighttime

Because i hated monsters

And dreaded scary movies

I hated blood and gory

It gave me nightmares

Traumatized whenever i heard screaming and frantic

Screeching from the television

Coming from my parent's room

They forgot that i was Afraid of the dark

Had to sleep with gospel music and a nightlight on

Hated when my mother would come into the room

Turn off the switch

Ignored my fears

Kiss my forehead goodnight

And whisper "you'll be fine

Just be brave

We'll never let anything harm you."

Here i am

Panicking as my brother lays in his bed across from me

My body starts to tremble

Voices of characters died

Had me shaking in my covers

I go to sleep

I wake up and watch a portal in the shape of a fireball

Appear on my wall

Chants of "join us, tre'" ricocheted in my room

I discovered i wasn't alone tonight

I was greeted by two hideous creatures

An Anomaly and a Fiend

Both disguised as robbers

Distorted and discolored like action figures

Who decided to take a seat on each side of my bed

I met the devil and insomnia

They extended their hands

In attempt to make acquaintance

Their voices,

Monotone and gloomy

I'm taken aback

Not sure what they wanted with me

Satan tells me he had a deal

In exchange,

It would cost me my soul

Me

Not understanding or comprehending

Why a proposition like this was made to me

Me

Being shown my life with wealth

Me

Looking at a depiction of what my latter years

Would be like with women, flashy cars, and power

Me

Feeling a tight hold on my body

Being told that I needed to make a decision today

Even though this was a dream

I wake up at 2am

Ran to the bathroom

After wetting the bed

I was scared and losing my mind

Cried as I sat on the toilet

Watching my tears fly off my face like raindrops

I disturbed my father's sleep

Told him what transpired

Asked him, "What do I do?"

"What do I say?"

"What words do I utter when I begin to pray?"

He told me "Tell him you're with God

And to get thee behind you

Don't worry about anything

God's going to see you through"

Me

Wanting to remain awake

Now I'm greeted with a hug by the Sandman

Paranoia contaminated my soul

Man, i couldn't catch a break

I yawned

Took a deep breath

Fell asleep

Me

I was being kidnapped!

I was dragged by my feet

My mouth was covered

No one

Not a single person

Could hear me scream out in torment

I couldn't escape their clutches

And here we are

In the garden of Eden

Such a beautiful sight to behold

The grass was much greener

Lilies and daffodils were in full bloom

The animals were gentle

I felt serenity and didn't want to leave

Fascinated I tell you

I took a couple steps forward

And watched

How this ethereal destination

Was only a mirage

A setting full of rainbows and peace

Transmuted to desolation and calamity

Me

Looking for a way to escape

Trying to find out

How I was going to get out of here

Now in a standoff with Satan

I couldn't run

When I went left

He followed

When I went right, he followed

He had a tight grip on me

I was stuck

I shouted

"What do you want from me?"

He chuckled

"I want you, Tre'.

Join me so that I don't have to hurt you"

BOOM!

There was a crack in the sky

A man came down from heaven

In a Flaming Chariot

Looking prolific and sublime

I was awestruck

I met Jesus

He called me by my name

Extended his arms out

And hugged me

He shown me my life

From a prominent view

His love made me feel brand new

I shook his hand

He told me "This is where you want to be

Now that you're in me, you'll have victory."

Satan yelled

"Tre', you're reckless I see

It's clear you made your decision

Well, I'm taking your soul any way

So here I come for the killing"

I shouted

"Yes, I'm with God

So get thee behind me

I rule you under my feet

Now you have to flee!"

He winds up his fireball

Ready to attack

Jesus stepped in

And told me to step back

He blocked it

Sent the devil back to where he came

He said "This isn't over tre'!

Watch me bring you trouble and shame!"

Jesus said "Troubles don't last anyways my brother

You're going to be just fine

Now go back to sleep

You need to be at school before 9."

Me

Waking up

Confident and content

Elated as I ate my breakfast

Reminded of the night when Jesus called me righteous

And the devil

Called me reckless.

REGRETS

Regret

Defined as feeling sad, repentant, or guilty

Over someone or something

That's happened or been done

Regret

Possessing damaging effects on the mind

And the body

When it turns into fruitless rumination

Regret

Is self blame

Regret

Is taking away hope

Regret

Is squeezing and suffocating the enjoyment

And fun out of every second

Every minute

Every hour

Every moment and memory one creates

Regret is denying yourself of happiness

And the desecration of the beauty of life

Do you have any regrets?

Do you have any "what if's?"

Do you regret missing that opportunity

Because you were invested in making others happy?

Do you regret giving yourself wholly to someone

Who only gave you a partial piece of them?

Do you regret loving the red flags out of a person?

Do you regret not taking that advice

About the person you decided to be with?

Instead, you find yourself picking up more broken pieces

And looking to other sources to heal your spirit?

Do you regret breaking the heart of someone

Who tried to love you

And you decided to build a wall up

To hide your emotions?

In order to not be considered weak?

A softy?

A sucker for love?

A hopeless romantic?

Do you regret giving up your body to a person

Who claimed to give you the world

Only to get their needs fulfilled?

And now you sit with a soul tie

That's impossible to break?

Do you regret missing out on your dreams

Because you have it fixated in your mind

That those dreams cannot be achieved?

Ladies and gentlemen

It's alright to raise your hands

In the midst of writing this poem

I stand before all of you

Full of regrets too

I regret not pouring into myself

Because I wanted to pour into everyone else

I regret confiding in certain people

Because they considered my venting sessions to be popcorn

And they consumed my pain as manna and comedy

I regret talking about suicide

I should've ran suicides on the court

Rather than plotting my demise

I regret not accepting who i am

I regret not following God's plan

I regret not going to therapy

And looking for quotes and messages

On facebook and instagram

I regret being public instead of private with my feelings

Regret not spending time with God

While he's been working hard

To rescue my life

I regret not writing this poem

But choosing to write diss poems

About myself

It's safe to say I regret, regret

That was then

This is now

I no longer depict myself

As anything negative

That people have said about me

I'm stronger than I've ever been

Now that I've put my confidence in God

I no longer regret anything

"Dear God,

Release what doesn't bring me peace

If it isn't adding to my life, subtract it

Burn every bridge that leads my life back to unhappiness

Burn every bridge that leads my life back to pain

Reveal what is real

Expose everything that isn't for me

Remind me that no hater can stop your favor

If I start to give up, remind me that I can always depend

On you

If I start to lose hope, remind me that your plans are

bigger than my dreams. In Jesus name, amen." (Trent Shelton)

Your favorite love poem

I found you

Opened my eyes to the windows of your heart

Created love on every page

You excite me

I found delight in your corneas

You listened as i strummed my pain with my words

Helped me discover beauty in the madness

The creativity in your lines

Allowed me to shine

In dark times

You held me

Cradled my feelings in your hands

Made it easy to compose poetry

Made it easy to compose stories

You're instrumental

A quintessential melody

Too melodic for the radio

I discovered things about myself

That revealed the sanctity of who I am

And that's because of you

You're my everything

You're love in human form

My church

My favorite worship song

My spark that sends radiant shockwaves

Throughout my body

I crown you queen of my universe

I crown you goddess of my galaxy

We grow and show growth

Melt in love and serendipity

Stand together side by side

And groove to our songs like marching bands

Conducted cosmos the atmosphere couldn't contain

We set the vibe because of our vibrations

And once our clothes came off

We danced to the rhythm of intimacy

Meshing like twin idyllic flames

Dripping off canvases with kisses to each crevasse

Bodies connected

Healed with each touch

Souls intertwining

Becoming equally yoked and unbreakable

You're magic

Music to my ears

My heartbeat

I'm nothing but a resounding cymbal

Without you

You're my breath that I take

Inhaling passion

Exhaling doubt

Watching and witnessing your melanin

Permeate my heart

And though the seasons may change

Situations may arise

No matter the weather or circumstances

Your love

Is what i desire

Our love

Is a place only meant for us to dwell

God gave us grace beyond the broken pieces

So it's only right

That i do the same

Hold me

As i hold you close

Lay your head on my shoulder

I'll be your protector

I'll be your teddy bear

When you cry

I'll always wipe the tears from your eyes

And let you know everything

Is going to be alright

I want to take credit

For when there's a smile on your face

You're my dream come true

Take my hand

Grab hold of me

Don't let go

Teach me your triggers

So I don't trigger you

Don't give up on me

I'm never giving up on you

I'm not here to control

I'm here to restore

As we rise

Continuing to soar like eagles wings

We'll remain together

Even after infinity

I love you

Signed,

Your favorite love poem.

As You Sleep

I wait in anticipation

For the moments when we

Can fall asleep

Whether we're together or on Facetime

Each moment is eclectic

I wait for you to go to sleep first

The sound of you breathing

Is refreshing

It calms and restores

The very depths of my soul

When you dream

I bask in the eminence of your beauty

It's easier to sleep

Knowing you're by my side

Nightmares are afraid

Of how peacefully you rest

Stars shimmer in praise

Remembering that I'll be waking up to you

The next day

I reminisce and smile

Fascinated by how we're in sync

And in tune

Our bodies connect

With the radiance of the moon

As you hold on to me

While your head rests against my chest

Remember that I'll always cover you

With my love

There's no place I'd rather be

I'll protect you

Keep you secure

Shield you from any thoughts of a bad dream

Even if we're not together

I'll never hang up

I'll stay awake while you continue to sleep

I pray

That your dreams are made reality

I PRAY

THERE'S A SMILE ON YOUR FACE

I'LL ALWAYS BE HERE

AS SOON AS YOU WAKE UP

IF THERE WERE TEARS

I'LL WIPE THEM AWAY

WILL NEVER GO TO BED UPSET WITH YOU

AND AFTER AN ARGUMENT

I'LL ALWAYS TELL YOU THAT I LOVE YOU

SHOWER ME WITH YOUR LOVE

I'LL RECIPROCATE

HOLD ME CLOSE

I PROMISE

I'LL NEVER LET YOU GO.

Sincerely Yours
(Souls Connected)

My heart beats for the two of us

Keeping a tight groove like steady drums

Preparing a melody for only us to experience

My song sings for the two of us

Angels compose verses of lyrics

That celebrates our love

My prayers are not only for me

But for you

For us

So that we rise

And shine bright like the sun

I want to hold you

Hold you beyond being physically intimate

Basking in your eminence and beauty

Hear the sound of you breathing as you sleep

I want to be that dream

You don't want to wake up from

Shower you in sentiments of sweet nothings

Keep you safe and secure

In my arms

I want you to be comfortable with me

I won't tell your secrets

Clothe me in your hugs

Dress me in your kisses

Let's mesh like twin flames

And set the world ablaze

With a love that's only exclusive

For the two of us

You

Yes you

You're Serenity in the flesh

You're Serenity in truth

The world stops and stares

At such a marvelous masterpiece

Sculpted in divine perfection

Unblemished

Cannot be desecrated by imperfections

Jealous minds and contradictions

Must acknowledge your royalty

I praise God for you

I crown you queen

Honoring you as your king

Letting you lead as I submit

And adhere to every need

Fulfilling them all to keep you at ease

You take my breath away

I'm fascinated how your life

Speaks rivers of testimonies

You can be weak around me

I be strong for the both of us

I'll carry the burdens

Hold your hand through the rain

We'll dance on our insecurities

We have the victory

Knowing our enemies are under our feet

Life is beautiful

Knowing that you're my significant other

I'll never hurt you

Because we got each other

I love you.

NO REHAB FOR HEARTBREAK

We met unexpectedly

Conversed as the sun went down

Smiles and love created synergy

Throughout the space

You took my hand

I gave you my heart

We instrumented an unbreakable connection

We

Two unlikely beings

Two people who had no intentions

Of being one

Became lovers who found joy beyond madness

Strummed our pain with melodies

Sung songs of devotion

United despite opposition

Distance didn't keep us apart

The fire we made brought us closer

Meshing like twin flames

Called each other by our nicknames

Only designed for us to know

Accepting the mission to love and grow

Made magic in the midst of tragedy

Conducted cosmos and streams of love

We were inseparable

You told me you loved me

I told you I'm never leaving

We orchestrated sweet music

As we transcribed our pain in hyperbole

You called me symphony

I called you poetry

Created an everlasting feeling

That was never meant to depart

Suddenly

You looked at me differently

As we came face to face

The connection started to fade

We shifted

You drifted

I was trying to play Mr. Fix It

Put blame on myself

Because I wanted us to work out

However

You chose the easy route

I thought love was supposed to go through the fire

Not be trapped by wires

I was risking it all

And gladly will

A chance with you

Is what I desire still

Poetry

You left my heart in disarray

You decided to leave

When I wanted you to stay

I was willing to change

What am I supposed to do without you?

There's no therapy for emptiness

No rehab for heartbreak

Loving you was no accident

I pray that you don't feel

Loving me was mistake

I wish

That I can trade all this back

For us to preserve what we had

I'll do anything to make you smile

Willing to work it out if you were mad

Praying that our love would be translucent

Forgive me if I was a nuisance

Now I'm left with memories

Ones that I'll hold dear

Waking and dreaming with a broken heart

Possessor of a fistful of tears

Yes poetry

I still love you

Even though you're no longer here.

OCTOBER 6TH

So I have four confessions about me

One, my name is not Tre, it's Lee

Two, I can be a know it all at times

Three, I claim to retire from poetry

But find myself writing new material

Four, I try my hardest to protect my heart

However, I've discovered that

I overly project my emotions

Recently, my brother and I had a heart to heart

He imparted this word of wisdom to me

"For true love to be formed

A piece of you must be removed

Love doesn't meet you where you're whole

Love meets you where you're broken

Love is seeing how much of someone's brokenness

You are willing to deal with

Love is love when our brokenness

Is addressed when we're around each other."

In the summer of 2021, I met love

My spirit was elated

My heart skipped beats

My eyes couldn't take my focus off of her

Love was phenomenal by design

Melted at the scent of A Thousand Wishes

Water in her words like oceanic winds

Love had my undivided attention

Morning text messages were effervescent

Late night phone conversations were soothing

We connected and bonded

Shared stories, laughter, and tears

Love called me hers

I called love mine

Never had a dull moment

Created poetry in our chemistry

United in the tapestry of prayer

We understood each other

Admitted we moved rapidly

But love kept us together

We were inseparable

Leading and submission was never a problem

We functioned as a team

She sung her song in melodious hyperbole

I fell awestruck before God

Wondering why it took Him so long

To bring me this angel

We grew harmoniously and individually

Had arguments and gave space when needed

Vowed that we'd come home to each other

Promised that we wouldn't change no matter what

Sadly,

Things started to shift

My insecurities got in the way

Love was in deep regret

For the mistakes she'd made

We drifted apart

Had to go our separate ways

Her absence tore me apart

I was going insane

Conversed with God every hour

Begging and pleading for Him

To bring her back

Concluded that she doesn't want to come home

Had to accept the fact

She no longer wants me

I wish I'd gave her more affirmations than accusations

I wish I listened to love

When she asked to take a break

I wish I was more private

Than public with my feelings

We'd probably would still be together

I wish love would still be here

Instead of giving up on me

And acting like I never existed

I'd give the whole me

To have her kisses and hugs

I'd trade my crown

To fall asleep and wake up next to her

I'd give everything I own

To see her smile again

But love taught me

That it's okay to be both messy and accepted

Vulnerability is strength

Love is not about staring at each other

But staring off in the same direction

Love is love when we can pick up each other's broken pieces

And construct a masterpiece

While being in the moment of life

So Dear Love,

I'm sorry for not taking the time to hear you

Thank you for reminding me of the king I am

I'm grateful for the queen you are

You helped me to find my smile

My faith in God is driven more boldly

I can finally release

What's been holding me back

Love, you are metal

You've been nuked thousands of times

But survived with all the scars to prove it

I was never expecting you to be perfect

I wanted you to be the missing puzzle piece

Inside my heart

To be honest

You still are

You still got me

Even though I no longer have you

Forgive me for all of my transgressions

I love you

More than mere melody

More than just saying those three words

Because I'd rather love you broken

So that we can heal

And be whole together

You taught me how to love

You're already my legacy

No one will take your place

As my muse

If this is truly goodbye

It was an honor to have met you

A privilege to know you

Hopefully one day

I'll have the opportunity to keep you again

You're my place of serenity

That's something you should always know

You're someone special

That I'll never let go

If you ever begin to cry

After hearing this poem

And you start to think about me

Your name is on two stars

That'll continue to shine bright

My diamond in the sky.

Your forever Bo.

THE BENEDICTION

Dear ex-love
As much as I want to hate you
Not wish you well
Not congratulate you on moving on
I hope you're at peace
I've concluded that we were
The best and worst parts of each other
My soul knew this wasn't good
Yet I chose to stay
Because I had hope that we'd still be together
I fervently prayed that we'd get back together
Begged and pleaded to have conversations
So that we can improve our relationship
However you chose to go in a different direction
My heart became the doormat that you chose to walk on
I was a target with your lasciviousness
Darting behind my back
You went from treating me like a king
To publicly making me a nuisance
And to this day I sit here wondering
How I could be this stupid
A picture has a thousand words
But you used your words for other pictures
That didn't involve me
I was a package
That was never meant to be dropped off at your door
You've shown me repeatedly that you didn't respect me
Created excuses for your mishandling of my heart
Where's the accountability?
Sometimes I wondered if you really cared about me
You called me your rock
But wanted a johnson that wasn't mine
And you chose it twice
Instead of staying by my side
You castrated love out of me
Concealed me in your web of lies

Oblivious to the tears that fell from my eyes
Yet claimed I sucked you dry of grace
And while I was persistent
In keeping my existence in your life
You ignored me
You told me that you didn't want me
You were in transition with moving on
On the day I needed you the most
You decided to let me go
When I continued to chase after you
You let me drown
When I wanted us to stay afloat
I still loved you
Even though you disconnected from me
HOW COME YOU DON'T LOVE ME ANYMORE?!
HOW COME I WASN'T ENOUGH FOR YOU?!
WHY WAS IT EASY FOR YOU TO SAY IT'S OVER?
I gave you your space
I gave you attention and time
Your betrayal doesn't come as a surprise
It's no longer new to me
If this was the cost of making memories
I've should've known better
I should've let you go sooner
I give up now
As much as I want to call you
Out of your name
Depict you as the villain
Disrespect and invalidate the feelings you "had" for me
It's not in me to be a monster
Part of the problem was that I did everything for you
I moved too fast
Rushed the process of dating
Ignored being your friend first
I disregarded the signs
I wanted you to be the love of my life
I died in my flesh because I was trying to save you
From your brokenness
But I should've left that job to God

I didn't want to forgive you
I didn't want to forgive someone who hurt me
And caused me pain
But I decided to trade my sorrows and shame
Chose to leave this pain and this poem on this stage
Surrendered my hurt and my heart to God
And I can finally say
I forgive you
I forgive you so that I can give you back to the world
And I'm not expecting an apology in return
I choose to forgive you
Not for you
But for me
So that I can finally be happy
And not be the hurt person
That hurts another person
Because of the damage you caused
It doesn't change what I've experienced
However this experience
Brought me closer to God
So I thank you
Thank you for memories
That I'll forever hold dear
This is how you destroy a generational curse
Put an end to a soul tie
Eliminating bitterness and rage
That still permeates in my veins
And along with releasing this impairment
I release you
I pray that what you've done to me
Doesn't happen to you
And by the time you realize my worth
I'll be worth more
I love you
Farewell, Ex Love
I pray you're happy and well
Signed
A King.

The Last Love Poem

When i first met you

I wondered how my eyes met yours

And felt guilty for staring at you

For too long

In that very moment

All i could muster up

Are comments in my mind

About how innocent your eyes look

Your voice soothes my soul

Like water across my ears

Your presence is nostalgic

You've made it easy to write poetry

I vow to take care of your heart

Even on the days

Where it seems

Like the light has disappeared

From all of the earth

If this were to be my last love poem to you

Let me start by saying

You'll always be my muse

You could never ruin a day or night

I'll still choose you after an argument or a fight

Because you are the light of my life

And no one is going to have that title

Except you

Your fragility is not a turn off but a turn on

Your broken pieces does not hinder your strength

It helps you to grow

I accept you

Even with the baggage you may still carry

If this were to be my last love poem to you

Know that I'll always still write you poetry

Praising God for making you

Acknowledging that you are an angel on earth

And I am so honored to have you

You're love in human form

Fortitude and confidence forms your divinity

You've taken a lot

Been through tremendous amounts of pain

Fallen down many times

But I adore the power in you getting up

If this were to be my last love poem to you

I want to tell you that you are truly a gift

You make every bone in my body stand straight

My heart beats songs of praise when you smile

When you wake up

And the sun rises

A sunset is in awe at how the rays kiss your skin

Heaven rejoices

Knowing that the queen you are

Is putting on her crown

Withstanding all of her opposition in excellence

If this were to be my last love poem to you

I knew I wanted to be with you

My body yearns for your touch

Submitting is never a challenge or difficult task

I WANT TO CONTINUE TO LEARN YOU

THE JOY THAT'S IN YOUR EYES

EVEN BEYOND THE MASCARA

MAKES MY WORLD FEEL SPECIAL

YOU'RE SERENE IN SERENITY

I CANNOT SEE A FUTURE

AND THIS PRESENT MOMENT

WITHOUT YOU IN MY LIFE

YOU MAKE ME FEEL ALIVE

IN MY ARMS YOU CAN FOREVER HIDE

I'LL NEVER TELL YOUR SECRETS

OR JUDGE YOU FOR YOUR MISTAKES

YES THERE WILL BE MOMENTS OF GIVING AND TAKING

BUT THE ONLY THING YOU GIVE AND TAKE FROM ME

IS MY AGAPE

A LOVE THAT WILL NEVER RUN OUT

ONLY MEANT FOR YOU

SO IF THIS IS MY LAST LOVE POEM TO YOU

LET ME TELL YOU THAT I'M HONORED TO BE YOUR KING

That it's a privilege to have you as my queen

That I want to shower you with flowers and rings

And listen to birds sing their melodies

I want to chase God

And continue to chase you

Reminding you that I'll never let you go

Watch as you sit on your throne

Beside me

You're Song of Solomon 1:5

Dressed in melanin

Crowned in glory

A majestic and magnificent portrait to behold

You're everything a queen should be

You're my prayer answered

My best friend

The perfect ending to this love story

And when we make love

I'll always tell you that it's yours

And no one

Will be able to have access to me

The way you do

I fulfill every desire

Without any hesitation

Because I'm here to serve you

If this is my last love poem to you

Know that I'll still pen you poetry

I don't want you to hate me

You can depict me as the monster to your friends

I'll take accountability

For the things I didn't do

But remember the good times we shared

The late night conversations that would have

Us falling asleep on the phone

If this were to be the last love poem to you

Think about how I took you to play laser tag

How you cheated in air hockey

The paintings we made and our writing sessions

Revisit the moments where we watched Bible study

Yes, you did most of the driving

But i made sure you had everything

And didn't stop until I knew you seen

The queen you are in the mirror

Reflect on the places we went

Like how we went to Mr. Crab on Valentine's Day

How couples starred at us

When we entered the restaurant

And they were in admiration

At how good we looked

Watching as we held hands

And in complete chemistry

Remember how we went to Via

To celebrate my birthday

How you promised that your love wouldn't change

And that you wouldn't go away

I'm still here

Even though you disappeared

So if this is my final love poem to you

I want you to print this out

And frame it

Tell your next boyfriend

That i apologize

And i wish that he didn't have to come into the picture

I want you to know

Despite all of our flaws

That meeting you and loving you

Was no accident

After all the times you've shown me

That you hated me

I still lie to myself

And say that it's love

Because if it wasn't

I wouldn't have the strength

To go on without you

You're the only one

Who can get away

With breaking my heart

So if this is my last love poem to you

I want you to know

That you deserve a relationship

With someone who doesn't make you compete

For affection

And never has you guessing

Where you stand with them

That's what i was trying to do

Forgive me

For not being the right man for you

I still depict you as the most beautiful woman

Of my galaxy

Despite the infidelity

So if this is my final love poem to you

Even if we don't cross paths

Or don't speak to each other again

I want you to know that I'm here for you

And that love will never end

Because no matter what

We'll always have each other

If this is my last love poem to you

Keep me forever etched in your heart

As you are in mine

And know from the deepest part of me

I love you.

Signed, your forever Bo.

ACKNOWLEDGEMENTS

Yo! We made it! We did it! Wooo!

Book twelve is now complete!

Man! This moment is surreal!

Now, to the best part of the book, the end credits!

First and foremost, THANK YOU GOD! Without YOU, I am NOTHING! All praises are to the Most High God! I love you, I give you all the glory, honor and praise because you deserve it!

Second, my parents! I love you both. Thank you for giving me life and introducing me to poetry. Both of you deserve your flowers!

My Brothers! Tyrone and Isaiah! I love y'all man! Keep pushing! It's up from here fellas! It's our time to shine and they are going to know the Brown name one way or another.

Jenny, I miss you sis! Rest in Power. I know your spirit is watching me and I wish you were here to see this! I love you!

My godchildren! Lord, Talaiya, Angaleen, Aamir, Dream, and Princey, I love you. God daddy is so proud to have all of you in

HIS LIFE. I GOT POETRY ABOUT ALL OF YOU THAT I'M GOING TO PUT OUT VERY SOON.

MY GODPARENTS! PAM AND MICHAEL WALTERS! I LOVE YOU!

MY FATHER IN MINISTRY PASTOR THOMAS A. MILLS, JR. MAN, I LOVE YOU SO MUCH! THANK YOU FOR EVERYTHING YOU'VE DONE FOR ME.

GRACE C.M.E. CHURCH, I APPRECIATE AND LOVE YOU!

ACACIA TAYLOR, TORRIE COOK, BRIANA WASHINGTON, LAUREN HARRIS, DANIELLE FOUNTAIN, DJ MEECHIE, ANGEL KIM, QUEEN FLOETRY, SHAYDON (KING SUAVEEE) HARRISON, MOJAVI EMI, KENYA AKA SONGBYRD, BEAUTIFUL BUTTERFLY, JANAIYA ON FIRE, MYSTIC, ALEX JACKSON, ANIKA JACKSON, SANDRENE HYLTON, AHMAAD ROBINSON, BRANDON LEAKE, DANIEL VALMONT, BRANDON JAMES, GLENN JOHNSON, TYRONE BRYAN, EARL MCCOY, EDMUND DUENKEL, SHARMONT "INFLUENCE" LITTLE, TYMANI RAIN, DEE TRUE POETRY, BALANC3, OSO, BROTHER BEAR, PHIL ALEXANDER, JENA FENTON, LETIF BELCHER, DJ D-DUB, SILENT QUILL, NBS MALAY, ADRIAN ELLIOT, CHANISE WILLIAMS-MCBRYDE, ROB AUGUSTINE, MIDNIGHT, AARON ST. LOUIS, CHIEF, SCOTT HARREL, NATE AND CHANEL GRAHAM, TARIQ SAINT-SANKOFA, MELIKIA COURTNEY, STINNAAA BABY, BINA,

The Lost Tribe of Poets, Miss Tiana Malcolm, Brandi Renee, The Honey Drippers Poetry Collective, Nick Austin, Nadiyah Renee, Kae Loe, Rudy, Krlwnd Sotto, Prince Ayinde, Artie Foxx, Infamous Lyricist, and all my clubhouse family I LOVE ALL OF YOU SO MUCH. THANK YOU FOR PUSHING MY PEN AND GIVING ME PROMPTS. YOU GUYS ARE ALL IMPACTFUL TO ME.

To mama Trician Salmon, I love you so much.

Sarah, thank you. Thank you for everything! It's always love and never bad blood. Keep poeting poet. I love you always. It's your time and I'm glad you're running your race with the baton!

To all my aunts, uncles, and cousins, thank you and love you.

To my niece Tiana! Man I love you so much babygirl and you're up next.

To YBG, Albi Besh!, EPC, Solace Family, and to the Fresh City Connection, We Made it! It's our time!

Thank you to every supporter and believer of my poetry!

I love you all so much...

— Lee "Tre" Brown, III (Tremaine Rashad) (Pyro)